H.A.P.P.Y.
A.N.N.I.V.E.R.S.A.R.Y.

Space for Personalized Message

Happy Anniversary: A Poem of Affection

ACRONYM POETRY GIFT SERIES

By Macarena Luz Bianchi

Illustrated by Zonia Iqbal

To receive a free ebook, exclusive content, more wonder, wellness, and wisdom, sign up for her *Lighthearted Living* e-newsletter at MacarenaLuzB.com and check out her other poems of self-expression, books, and projects.

ISBN: Hardcover: 978-1-954489-08-0 | Paperback: 978-1-954489-10-3 | Ebook: 978-1-954489-09-7

Imprint

Spark Social, Inc. Miami, FL, USA, SparkSocialPress.com

Ordering Information: Licensing, custom books, and special discounts are available on quantity purchases. For details, contact the publisher at info@sparksocialpress.com.

H.A.P.P.Y. A.N.N.I.V.E.R.S.A.R.Y.

A Poem of Affection

ACRONYM POETRY GIFT SERIES

Macarena Luz Bianchi

Imprint
Spark Social Press

H.A.P.P.Y. A.N.N.I.V.E.R.S.A.R.Y.

Happy Anniversary my lover, my life, my love!

Always cherish our affection.

Proud of who we are:

Playful, passionate, and present.

You are profoundly loved every day, and
especially today, on our special day!

Another fantastic year together.

Now we get to celebrate.

Never stop loving you
and the life we make.

I adore and appreciate every
moment of every day.

Vibrant are my days, thanks
to the love we create.

Every day is fun and new
when I spend it with you.

Remember how we met?
Our first kiss? Our love story?

Soulmate, your kiss
is bliss, and our precious
bond thrills me.

Another year together for us to thrive and flourish.

Romantic and resilient, we
make it through any storm
and enjoy the weather.

You are mine, and I am yours...

Happy Anniversary
my lover, my life, my love!

H.A.P.P.Y. A.N.N.I.V.E.R.S.A.R.Y.

A POEM OF AFFECTION

Happy Anniversary my lover, my life, my love!

Always cherish our affection.

Proud of who we are:

Playful, passionate, and present.

You are profoundly loved every day, and especially on our special day!

Another fantastic year together.

Now we get to celebrate.

Never stop loving you and the life we make.

I adore and appreciate every moment of every day.

Vibrant are my days, thanks to the love we create.

Every day is fun and new when I spend it with you.

Remember how we met? Our first kiss? Our love story?

Soulmate, your kiss is bliss, and our precious bond thrills me.

Another year together for us to thrive and flourish.

Romantic and resilient, we make it through any storm and enjoy the weather.

You are mine, and I am yours... Happy Anniversary my lover, my life, my love!

࿇ ☙✦❧ ࿇

Thank you, Dear Reader!

Get Inspired & Stay Connected

To receive a free ebook, exclusive content, more wonder, wellness, and wisdom, sign up for her Lighthearted Living e-newsletter at MacarenaLuzB.com and check out her other poems of self-expression, books, and projects. ✨

Your Feedback is Appreciated

If you like this book, please review it to help others discover it. If you have any other feedback, please let us know at info@macarenaluzb.com or via the contact page at MacarenaLuzB.com. We would love to hear from you and know which topics you want in the next books. 🌻

About the Author

Macarena Luz Bianchi has a lighthearted and empowering approach and is affectionally considered a Fairy Godmother by her readers. Beyond her collection of gift books and poems, she writes screenplays, fiction, and non-fiction for adults and children. She loves tea, flowers, and travel.

Subscribe to her *Lighthearted Living* newsletter for a free ebook and exclusive content at MacarenaLuzB.com and follow her on social media. 💞

Macarena Luz Bianchi

Gift Book Series

ACRONYM POETRY COLLECTION

- *Be My Valentine: A Poem of Love*
- *Congratulations: A Poem of Triumph*
- *Friendship: A Poem of Appreciation*
- *Happy Birthday: A Poem of Celebration*
- *Intimacy: A Poem of Adoration*
- *Sympathy: A Poem of Solace*

With more to come including: *Encouragement, Graduation*, and so on.

POETRY COLLECTION

- *Glorious Mom: A Poem of Appreciation*
- *Gratitude Is: A Poem of Empowerment*
- *Gratitude Is: Poem & Coloring Book*
- *The Grateful Giraffes: What is Gratitude?*

Also available for children and in Spanish:
Colección de Poesía I.

www.ingramcontent.com/pod-product-compliance
Lightning Source LLC
Chambersburg PA
CBHW042335030426
42335CB00027B/3351